D1288732

Fact Finders®

DISGUSTING JOBS
DURING THE CIVIL WAR

THE DOWN AND DIRTY DETAILS

BY ANITRA BUDD

Content Consultant:
Jamie Bronstein, PhD, Professor of History,
New Mexico State University

CAPSTONE PRESS
a capstone imprint

Fact Finders Books are published by Capstone Press,
1710 Roe Crest Drive, North Mankato, Minnesota 56003
www.mycapstone.com

Library of Congress Cataloging-in-Publication Data
Names: Budd, Anitra, author.
Title: Disgusting jobs during the Civil War : the down and dirty details / by Anitra Budd.
Description: North Mankato, Minnesota : Capstone Press, 2018. | Series: Fact finders. Disgusting jobs in history
| Includes bibliographical references and index. | Audience: Age 8-10. | Audience: Grade 4 to 6.
Identifiers: LCCN 2017038583 (print) | LCCN 2017039106 (ebook) | ISBN 9781543503715 (eBook PDF) | ISBN
9781543503678 (hardcover)
Subjects: LCSH: United States—History—Civil War, 1861-1865—Social aspects--Juvenile literature. | United
States—History—Civil War, 1861-1865—Juvenile literature.
Classification: LCC E468.9 (ebook) | LCC E468.9 .B886 2018 (print) | DDC 973.7/1—dc23
LC record available at https://lccn.loc.gov/2017038583

Editorial Credits
Editor: Alyssa Krekelberg
Designer: Maggie Villaume
Production specialist: Laura Manthe

Photo Credits
Alamy: Chris Pondy, 16–17, Scott Camazine, 22, Steven Sommers, 12; iStockphoto: Carmine Salvatore, 13,
DenGuy, 9, FlamingPumpkin, cover (left), kschulez, cover (bottom), lenalir, 13 (bucket); North Wind Picture
Archives, 4, 5 (top and bottom), 17, 21, 24–25; Shutterstock Images: aphichato, cover (top right), Asmus
Koefoed, 28, ESB Basic, 18–19, Everett Historical, 6–7, 14, 26–27, 29, Luchenko Yana, 5 (background), Maria
Chavdarova Mavrona, 15, Mark C. Morris, 23, Protasov AN, 11, Surapol Usanakul, 10, Visual Cortex, 8

Design Elements: iStockphoto, Shutterstock Images, and Red Line Editorial

Printed and bound in Canada.
010800S18

TABLE OF CONTENTS

THE SICKENING
CIVIL WAR

The Civil War (1861–1865) divided the United States. Northern and Southern states could not agree on how to run the country. The biggest issue that split the Confederacy in the South and the Union in the North was slavery. In the South, farmers forced enslaved people to work in the fields, care for children, cook, and clean. Most people in the South thought the government should allow slavery to continue.

The North and South had many differences. But one thing they had in common was that people had to work. There were lots of jobs to do during the war. Many of these jobs were hard, dirty, and gross.

APRIL 12–14, 1861
The first battle of the Civil War takes place at Fort Sumter in South Carolina. Confederates fire on Union forces.

APRIL 6–7, 1862
Two laundresses are killed during the Battle of Shiloh while running away from the fighting.

JULY 1–3, 1863
The Battle of Gettysburg takes place in Gettysburg, Pennsylvania. By the end of the battle, more than 51,000 soldiers are killed, wounded, captured, or missing.

JULY 6, 1864
Approximately 400 Confederate prisoners of war arrive at the Elmira prison camp in Elmira, New York.

AUGUST 1864
The Andersonville prison camp in Andersonville, Georgia, holds its largest number of Union prisoners at one time: 33,000.

Prisoners lived in horrible conditions in war camps.

BATTLE OF GETTYSBURG (1863)

ELMIRA

BATTLE OF ANTIETAM (1862)

BATTLE OF BULL RUN (1861)

UNITED STATES OF AMERICA

BATTLE OF SHILOH (1862)

CONFEDERATE STATES OF AMERICA

BATTLE OF CHANCELLORSVILLE (1863)

ANDERSONVILLE

FORT SUMTER (1861)

BATTLE OF VICKSBURG (1863)

ABOMINABLE ARMY

Nearly 3.5 million soldiers fought in the Civil War. The Union Army had about 2.7 million people, and at least 750,000 people joined the Confederate fighting forces. A soldier's main job was to fight, but most didn't spend much time on the battlefield. Their days were filled with practice drills, long marches, and shared chores like cleaning the camp.

Confederate soldiers tried to drive Union forces out of Atlanta, Georgia, in 1864.

Army camps were filled with soldiers and animals. They created stinking piles of poop.

Wind and rain spread waste around the camp. The soldiers' food and water supplies could become **contaminated**. These bits of waste were usually too small to see. This meant soldiers often didn't know they were eating a helping of poop with every meal.

Soldiers sometimes wore their uniforms for weeks at a time without washing them. Muddy hikes and bloody battles made their clothes ragged and smelly.

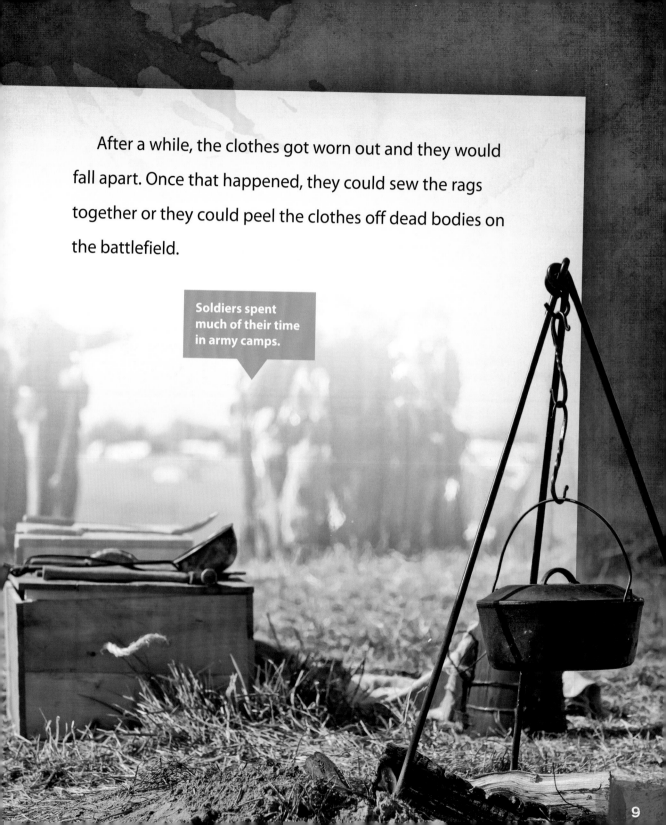

After a while, the clothes got worn out and they would fall apart. Once that happened, they could sew the rags together or they could peel the clothes off dead bodies on the battlefield.

Soldiers spent much of their time in army camps.

Finding clothes wasn't the worst of the soldiers' problems. In the South, mosquitoes bit the soldiers all day long. Lice made homes in soldiers' hair. The insects crawled on their arms and legs. They were even in the soldiers' underwear.

Soldiers thought of many ways to get rid of the pests. They tried boiling their clothes and wore their uniforms inside out. The most common way soldiers killed lice was by picking them out of their clothes. They crushed them between their fingers. Once, a soldier picked 52 lice out of one shirt.

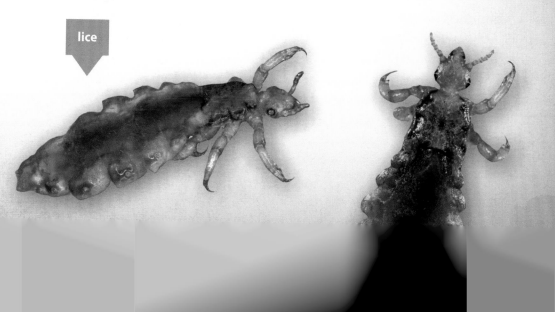

lice

LOUSY LAUNDRY

Many soldiers had to deal with filthy uniforms. But some had clean laundry. Getting uniforms clean wasn't easy, though. It involved cutting up animal bodies and stirring a boiling pot of blood, fat, and chemicals for hours.

Laundresses traveled with both armies. Some laundresses took the job because their husbands or sons were part of a **company**. Others wanted to serve their country. Some were enslaved. They were forced into the job against their will.

Doing laundry in the Civil War was sweaty work. Laundresses had to clean dozens of uniforms at a time. Most uniforms were blood-stained. They were also bursting with lice. Each load usually took three or four days to finish.

company — group of soldiers, usually consisting of one to two platoons

FOUL FACT

Soldiers who couldn't afford laundry service boiled their clothes in mess kettles. These were the same pots they used to cook their food.

Laundresses spent a lot of their time standing over tubs of steaming, scummy water.

In the 1800s most laundresses made their soap from three ingredients: water, animal fat, and a chemical called **lye**. The fat came from dead animals. The animal's body would be cut open. The white, bloody fat was taken from the animal's muscle. The fat went into a big iron pot. Water and lye were added. Lye washed away the dirt and blood that stained clothes, but lye is very harsh. It can burn skin and it even causes blindness if it gets in a person's eyes.

lye — substance made by soaking ashes and wood in water; used in making detergents and soap

DEAR DIARY

Once the fat, water, and lye were mixed together, the laundress started a fire underneath the pot. She stirred the stinking goop with a big spoon or stick. The soap would thicken. The laundress poured it into another pot. She let it cool and harden until it was ready to use.

It takes hours to make handmade soap.

CHAPTER THREE

MISERABLE MEDICINE

Ammunition used during the war did horrible damage. Lead balls shattered bones. They left large, gaping wounds. If a soldier was hit in the arm or leg, the limb was sometimes **amputated**. Doctors performed almost 30,000 amputations during the Civil War.

Minié balls were a type of bullet used during the Civil War.

ammunition — objects fired from guns

amputate — to cut off someone's arm, leg, or other body part, usually because the part is damaged

To remove a limb, the doctor first gave the patient **anesthesia**, which made patients sleepy and calm. If a doctor didn't have anesthesia, his assistants held down the kicking and screaming patient. The doctor cut into the limb with a small knife. He used that cut as a guide. Then he hacked off the limb with a saw. This sent skin, blood, and bone flying everywhere. The limb would fall off.

anesthesia — liquid, gas, or injection that prevents pain during treatments and operations

Then the doctor scraped the end of the bone until it was smooth. This kept the bone from poking through the skin. After that he would let the wound scab up.

Doctors also sewed flaps of loose skin over wounds with a needle and thread. The thread was often made from horsehair or sheep guts.

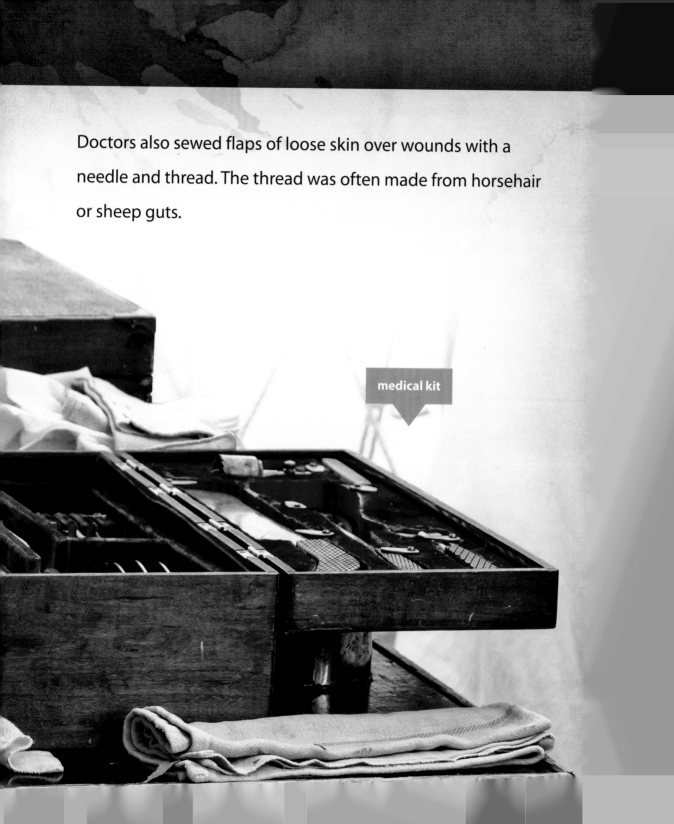

medical kit

DEAR DIARY

"Began my visits among the Camp Hospitals in the Army of the Potomac. Spent a good part of the day in a large brick mansion, on the banks of the Rappahannock, used as a Hospital since the battle—Seems to have receiv'd only the worst cases. Out doors, at the foot of a tree, within ten yards of the front of the house, I notice a heap of amputated feet, legs, arms, hands. . . . Several dead bodies lie near, each cover'd with its brown woollen blanket. In the door-yard, towards the river, are fresh graves."

—*Walt Whitman, poet and Union nurse,* 1862

Dirt, sweat, spit, and blood got into wounds and infected them. The infected wounds oozed pus. If the pus was creamy and white, doctors thought the wound was getting better. They only worried if the pus was bloody, watery, and smelly, but all pus is a sign of infection. Doctors poured acid on the wounds because they wanted to burn away the infection. Soldiers cried out in pain.

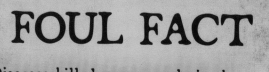

FOUL FACT

Diseases killed more people in the Civil War than knives, guns, or cannons. For every three soldiers killed in battle, five more died from a disease.

Nurses helped take care of patients during the Civil War.

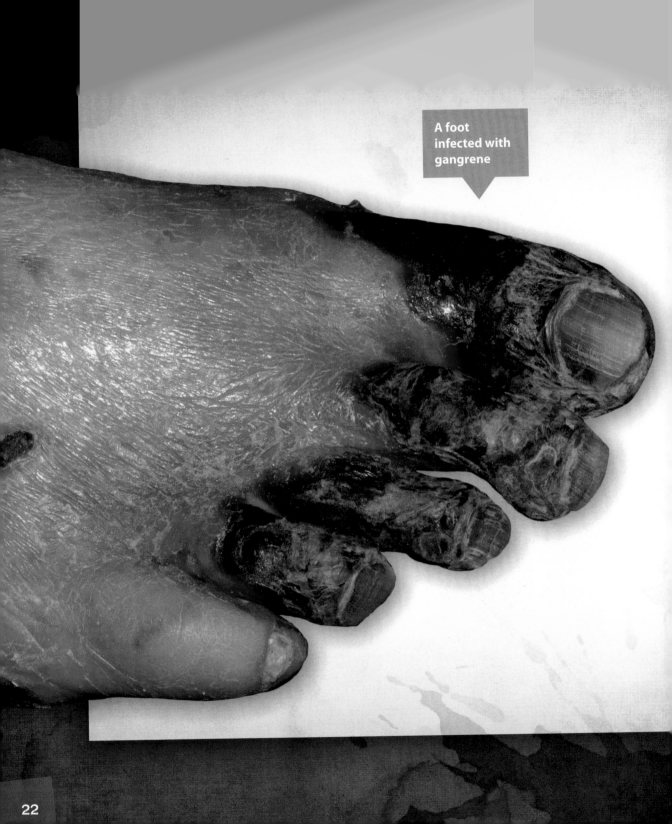

A foot
infected with
gangrene

One of the worst kinds of infections was **gangrene**. No one knew what caused it, but everyone knew how terrible it was. When a wound was infected with gangrene, the skin around it began to stink. The skin eventually turned black and died. The infection spread fast. Sometimes it spread up to half an inch (1.3 cm) every hour. A soldier could sometimes watch his flesh melt away before his eyes.

gangrene — condition in which the skin decays, usually because the blood supply is cut off to that part of the body

CHAPTER FOUR

PUTRID PRISONS

When soldiers were captured, they were sent to prison camps. In the worst camps, thousands of men were crammed together in tight spaces. Flies, lice, and poop were everywhere. What little food there was often had maggots and other insects crawling inside.

Prisoners didn't receive much food during the Civil War.

Guards were assigned to watch over the prisoners. These men were not always trained soldiers. This meant they had to guard men who knew much more about fighting than they did.

They were also outnumbered and poorly armed.
Even so, most prisoners were no threat to guards. They were
too weak from starvation and disease.

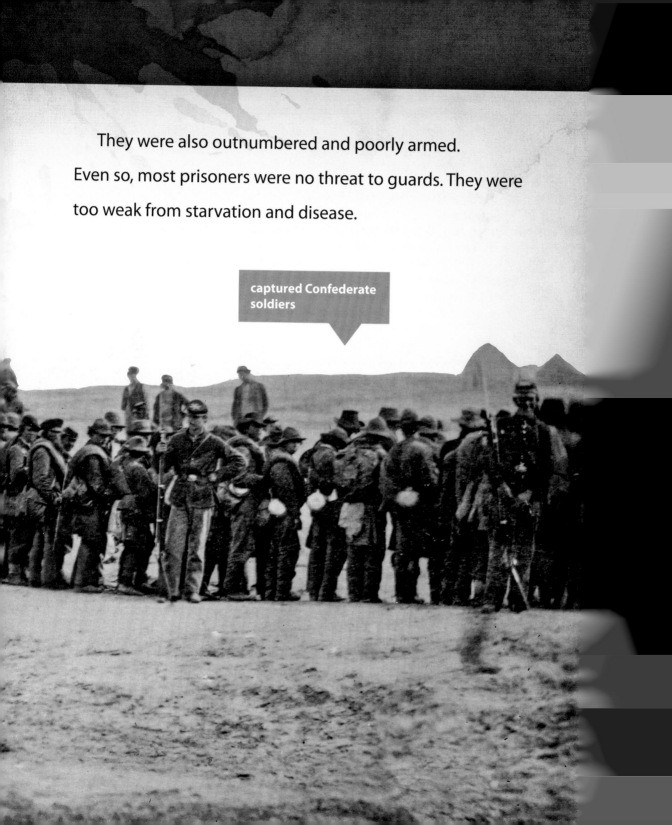

captured Confederate soldiers

Prisons were harsh in the North and the South. Prisoners had filthy rags for clothes and their skin was black with dirt and dried blood. They reeked of body odor. The prisoners pooped and urinated in the same place they got their drinking water. This spread **dysentery**, which gave prisoners constant diarrhea. During the winters up north, many prisoners had only their tattered clothes for warmth. Sometimes men got **frostbite**. They had to have their frozen limbs cut off.

ns were used on
e prisoners of war.

dysentery — a sometimes deadly infection of the intestines that can cause diarrhea
frostbite — when tissue is damaged from very cold temperatures

NASTY BUT NECESSARY

Ghastly wounds, wriggly maggots, and steaming piles of poop—men and women who worked during the Civil War saw these and many more disgusting sights. Soldiers fought lice and disease in the army camps. Laundresses stirred pots of boiling fat for hours. Doctors and nurses performed thousands of amputations and prison guards witnessed some of the worst conditions of the war. Work during the Civil War was disgusting, but the workers in the Confederacy and the Union were willing to go to any lengths. They thought their way of life was at stake.

GLOSSARY

ammunition (am-yoo-NISH-uhn) — objects fired from guns

amputate (AM-pyoo-tayt) — to cut off someone's arm, leg, or other body part, usually because the part is damaged

anesthesia (an-is-THEE-zhuh) — liquid, gas, or injection that prevents pain during treatments and operations

company (KUHM-puh-nee) — group of soldiers, usually consisting of one to two platoons

contaminated (kuhn-TAM-uh-nay-tid) — dirty or unfit for use

dysentery (DYS-uhn-tair-ee) — a sometimes deadly infection of the intestines that can cause diarrhea

frostbite (FRAWST-bite) — when tissue is damaged from very cold temperatures

gangrene (GANG-green) — condition in which the skin decays, usually because the blood supply is cut off to that part of the body

lye (lie) — substance made by soaking ashes and wood in water; used in making detergents and soap

READ MORE

Ablard, Michelle. *The Civil War: Brother against Brother*. Huntington Beach, Calif.: Teacher Created Materials, 2017.

Spinner, Stephanie. *Who Was Clara Barton?* New York: Grosset & Dunlap, 2014.

Thompson, Ben. *Guts & Glory: The American Civil War*. New York: Little, Brown and Company, 2014.

INTERNET SITES

Use FactHound to find internet sites related to this book

Visit *www.facthound.com*

Type in this code: 9781543503678

CRITICAL THINKING QUESTIONS

1. Imagine you're thinking about becoming a laundress during the Civil War. How would you make your decision?

2. Why do you think many soldiers stayed in the army and lived in the dirty camps? Explain your reasoning.

3. Civil War nurses had to be neat, serious, and healthy. What other qualities do you think would have made for a good Civil War nurse?

INDEX

ABOUT THE AUTHOR

Anitra Budd is a writer, editor, and educator. She has written books and articles for young people and adults. She enjoys reading, sewing, and learning new languages.